Virginia Treasures

Amazing Places

in the Commonwealth

By David Messick

Original Illustrations by Cory Steiger

Virginia Treasures
Amazing Places in the Commonwealth

Text and Original Photos: David Messick
Illustrations: Cory Steiger

Second Printing / Printed in the USA
ISBN: 979-8-9893939-0-9
Rainbow Puppet Publications
18 Easthill Court
Hampton, Virginia 23664
Rainbow Puppet Productions is a non-profit, educational, entertainment company.

www.rainbowpuppets.com

Designed by Virginia Gabriele

Puppets included in this book were created by Laura Baldwin, Jill Harrington, Frank Lakus.

Rainbow Puppeteers include James Cooper, Wesley Huff, Alyssa Jones, Silas McKinney, David and Joshua Messick.

Thanks to
Traci Massie, Erin Matteson, Curtis Johnson, Sentara Health Plans, Tony Gabriele, David & Stephanie Messick, Marcy Messick, Nancy Kent Swilley, and Rose West.

Dedicated to the memory of
Mel T. Brooks
One of our first puppeteers, my childhood friend,
and a treasure to everyone he met

Contents

Caverns of Virginia 6

Natural Bridge 24

Natural Tunnel....................................... 36

Natural Chimney 42

Fairy Stone Park 48

The Dismal Swamp 56

The Great Falls..................................... 64

The Chesapeake Bay............................ 71

A Final Word... 80

Partial Bibliography 82

Thanks 82

Glossary... 83

Rainbow Puppet Books 84

Foreword

When I think of treasure, I often think of gold, diamonds, and other gems. All of them are valuable. But what about another kind of treasure? What about the one-of-a-kind locations that you can see once then remember forever? I think there are many such locations all over Virginia. Please join me as we find breathtaking treasure scattered from one end of the state to the other.

The sun rises on the Chesapeake Bay.

Virginia Caverns

It was a warm Sunday afternoon in 1884, but it was about to get a lot cooler. Alfred and Elmer Neff were playing on the newly-created rock pile near their home. Their father, Abraham, is like most other farmers in the area. He was happy that the railroad tracks would carry trains right by his home. He hoped that it would allow him to sell more of his fruits and vegetables to people up and down the rail line. He was more than happy to let the railroad workers search for the rocks they need for the train line.

Alfred yelled to his brother, "Hey, you be careful jumping around on those rocks. Dad'll be awful angry if you get hurt playing around."

As soon as he said these words, Elmer slipped on one of the rocks busted up by the railroad workers.

"Elmer! Are you okay?" cried Alfred as he got close.

There was silence for a moment. Then Elmer finally spoke. "I think I found something."

"We found that you can't stand up on your own two feet," said Alfred.

"No. Come here, I feel something. Cold air… coming out of these rocks," said Elmer.

The Neff family sits near the original cave opening. *(Shenandoah Caverns archives)*

Alfred felt it, too; cool air blowing out from the rock pile. "It's coming out from under this big rock. Get up and help me move it."

The two worked together to move one big rock, and then another, and then another. Soon they uncovered a dark, deep hole with cold air coming out. They strained to see anything.

"It must be awful deep," said the younger brother.

Alfred jumped up. "There's only one way to find out!"

"God only knows what's down there … and that's fine by me. Remember how sometimes we see smoke coming out of holes in the ground?" asked Elmer.

Alfred shook his head, "In the winter?"

Elmer added, "A girl in school told me that's the devil himself down there!"

"Now you're letting some girl in school scare you out of having a real adventure. Go in the house and get some candles out of the cupboard. I'm getting that long rope out of the barn."

They tied the rope around the strongest nearby tree. Alfred held on to the other end ready to make his way down the hole.

Elmer was still scared, but he was also excited. He was glad that his older brother had so much courage. Soon Alfred had disappeared in the darkness. Only the occasional sound of small rocks falling down the hole and the shifting of the rope told Elmer

his brother was still okay.

Finally, the sounds stopped. "I think I've hit the bottom. It's okay down here. Now it's your turn, Elmer."

He took a deep breath and started down the hole to join his older brother. Soon he was there in the darkness and was glad he could feel his brother by his side.

By the candle glow they could finally see the amazing wonder right under their farm. They saw a giant underground ballroom made of rock. Hanging up high were strange formations clinging to the ceiling. They looked like icicles, but they were made of rock. Down the way, they saw columns, like those on a porch. But these columns weren't wooden; they were made of rock as well. Water clung to some of

These folds and curves are called "Bacon" formations.

the rocks, and in other places it dripped to the ground. The droplets sparkled in the candlelight, making the room seem all the more magical.

It was hard to take it all in. The two boys kept turning in a slow circle taking in the view. As wonderous as it was, Elmer was glad to hear the next thing out of Alfred's mouth.

"We better head back up. There are dark tunnels in every direction. Dad'll know what to do."

And their dad did know what to do. It was 1884 when the boys discovered the cave right underneath the farm. The family explored away, finding room after room of amazing underground beauty.

Word spread of their find and with rail travel now underway, the family sold the property to a local businessman. By 1922 a three-story lodge was built, and Shenandoah Caverns opened to the public.

Over 100 years later, it is still open and still one of the most beautiful caverns in the state.

The Shenandoah Caverns pixie has welcomed visitors for generations.

Always Cool

On a recent summer visit to Shenandoah Caverns, the electric sign at the nearby high school warns that it's 101 degrees outside … and it feels like it. Yet, inside the caverns, the thermometer reads 51 degrees. Being underground, summer or winter, the caverns remain around 51 to 54 degrees.

On a really hot day, after being outside working or playing, it sure is nice to step inside an air-conditioned building. Nothing can beat that cool flowing air when you're hot and sweaty. But indoor air conditioning is a fairly new idea.

Before the time of air conditioning, a great way to beat the heat was a visit to a local cavern. No wonder summer dances, weddings, and other events were frequently held in many of the caverns.

How do caves form?

It takes water and time to form a cave. Underground rivers and water trickling down from the surface slowly wash away limestone and clay. This constant washing away of stone leaves caverns like Shenandoah. It is water that also creates the breathtaking formations inside. Water seeps into the cavern and begins to drip to the ground. Small particles of lime in the water are left on the ceiling and down below. They create the stalactites on the ceiling and the stalagmites on the floor.

With giant columns and formations all around, being created one drop of water at a time, one small particle of lime at a time, it takes centuries to create huge formations. Simple formations like the fragile "soda straw" hangings can grow a third of an inch in one year. Other formations can take much longer.

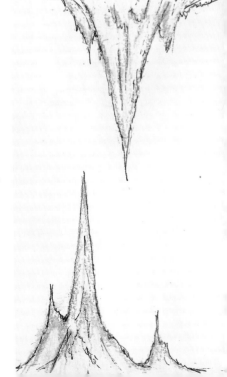

To remember the difference between the two formations, remember that

- A stalac<u>tite</u> holds TIGHT to the ceiling.
- You MIGHT trip on a stala<u>gmite</u>.

Other Caverns in Virginia...

Shenandoah Caverns were not the first commercial "show caves" to open to the public in Virginia. There are many others, and each has a story to tell.

Grand Caverns

Grand Caverns was first opened to the public as Weyer's Cave in 1806. It is the oldest continuously operating "show cave" in America. During the Civil War, both Union and Confederate soldiers visited. Many signed their names on the cave walls. In order to protect Virginia caves, it is now against the law to sign the walls or touch the formations.

Writing on the walls is now forbidden. Some of these signatures go back to the time of the Civil War.

Candlelight tours were popular at Grand Caverns in the 1800s. *(public domain)*

The original public tours were conducted by candlelight. The caverns have restarted this practice, offering candle tours on select evenings.

This giant oyster shell formation is called a cave shield. It is estimated that the bottom of this shell weighs one ton. Grand Caverns has over 500 cave shields. Only Lehman's Cave in Nevada has as many.

Skyline Caverns

While Shenandoah Caverns was found by two brothers playing in a rock pile left by railroad workers, it was the mass use of the automobile that caused a different kind of explorer to find and open Skyline Caverns in Front Royal. In 1931, plans were made to create a scenic road along the Blue Ridge Mountains of Virginia. The road would provide wonderful vacation opportunities for people to visit Virginia's mountains. The construction would provide work for many Americans who were struggling to support their families during the Great Depression. This was a time when work and money were hard to find.

Rare anthodite formations are found in only a few locations in America and one in France. *(Shutterstock)*

Since Front Royal was the northern starting point for the Skyline Drive, geologist Walter S. Amos was hired to try to find a show cave in the Front Royal area. He found such a cave after discovering a sinkhole. This led to the excavation and opening of the caverns in 1939.

The caverns are especially noted for their rare anthodite formations. These are six-sided crystals made of calcite. These rare formations are found in a few caves in America and one cave in France.

Just as the trains had opened up Shenandoah Caverns to tourists, the opening of Skyline Drive created a whole new way for Americans to travel and see amazing sites in Virginia.

Netting helps protect the formations from damage.

The formations seen at the bottom of this picture are actually a reflection, seen in the "Dream Lake."

Luray… Where Rocks Can Sing

The largest cavern in the eastern United States is Luray Caverns. While Native Americans knew of the caverns long ago, it was discovered by Europeans in 1878 and has become one of the most popular attractions in the state. In 2018, it was estimated that half a million people visit the site each year.

Luray is noted for its Giant's Hall with a 47-foot column, its Dream Lake which creates a mirror image of the formations above, the Fried Egg formation that really does look like the breakfast food, and its Stalacpipe Organ. Advertisements on billboards across

The fried egg formation looks almost good enough to eat.

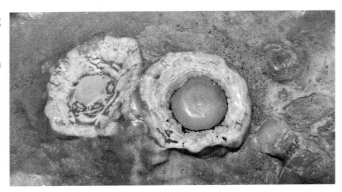

the state would say "Hear Rocks Sing!" as an invitation to the location.

Tiny hammers are wired to hit selected stalactites scattered throughout the caverns. These hammers are activated by a giant organ that sits on a pedestal. While there are many keys and pedals on the organ, the instrument actually plays 37 carefully tuned stalactites.

According to Luray Caverns, the Great Stalacpipe Organ is the world's largest musical instrument.

Tiny hammers strike stalactites scattered throughout the caverns. *(Luray Caverns)*

The Cave that Almost Didn't Open

Down the road, we find a treasure that almost didn't open to the public. The Caverns at Natural Bridge were discovered in the 1890s. As the deepest cave on the East Coast, there was hope that it would be a great added attraction for folks visiting the Natural Bridge. Men began excavating and exploring the cave to determine where interesting paths could be opened for the general public.

All was fine, until the men found a dark pit. Their ever-present lanterns weren't bright enough to see the bottom. The men became determined to find out how deep the hole was. Grabbing some pots and pans, they leaned forward and dropped them into the darkness. For a while, there was silence ... as if the hole really had no end. Then, they heard what they had expected, a series of clanks as the pots found the rock bottom of the cave.

What they heard next was not at all what they expected. From the deep hole, they heard a loud scream of ... was it a woman? Was it something else? It was a high-pitched unstoppable moan. The sound kept coming, echoing and bouncing throughout the

(Shutterstock)

deep, dark cave.

It finally became unbearable. One man dropped his lamp. As their shadows made strange images on the cave walls, the men ran up to the surface, never to return.

Some people believe this story is fact. Others

Was this gate outside the Caverns at Natural Bridge placed to keep people out or to keep something in?

believe it's just a legend. You can decide for yourself. But as you decide, try to answer these questions:

First, why did it take almost 90 years before anyone attempted to open those caverns to the public?

Second, as they were preparing paths in 1978, why did they find a rusted lamp, a lamp an explorer wouldn't leave behind for any reason, right beside the deep pit?

You can see the lamp in a display case at the cave's entrance. It's a final warning before you dare explore the Caverns of Natural Bridge.

The lantern that was left by explorers. *(Jennifer Shanks)*

The Natural Bridge of Virginia

There's a legendary tale that has been passed down through the Native American Monacan Nation from generation to generation. Their warriors have been overpowered by their enemy, the Algonquins. The Monacans have been chased through the countryside all night long. Even the rising sun offers no hope. A fog has rolled in and with limited ability to see, the fighters have lost their way. How will they escape? How will they find their way home? The enemy is coming closer and closer. No longer able to rely on their remaining strength and skills, they stop and pray for renewed courage and a clear path home.

As they open their eyes, they cannot believe the sight that appears. The fog rises like a curtain to reveal a giant mountain in front of them, with a passage underneath and a bridge above that can return them safely home. In their mind, this natural bridge is nothing short of a miracle sent in answer to prayer. It gives them the courage and strength to fight and win their battle. At the end of their fight, the bridge gives them a safe, and forever sacred, path back home.

This is the reason the Monacan Nation holds the grounds surrounding the Virginia Natural Bridge so dear, even to this day. But it's not just the Monacans that stand in awe of this amazing site. The Natural Bridge has attracted and thrilled visitors from around the world.

How Was It Made?

As we learned earlier with the formation of caves, water can seep underground to create openings and passages under the earth. Sometimes those passages are actually underground rivers that washed away limestone. It is believed that the Natural Bridge was once part of a huge underground cavern. The water eventually washed away the upper ceiling of much of the cave. All that remained was the huge Natural Bridge formation that can be seen today.

The nearby Caverns at Natural Bridge are a very wet and active caverns system, which shows just how effective water can be in transforming and "eating away" at rock. Inside, you can see dark sections of deposits that were once an ocean floor. In this "floor" you can find fossils of sea life including oysters and urchins.

Limestone is created by the shells and other remains of ancient sea life. Drops of water inside caves can pick up traces of limestone which slowly build up the formations on the floors and ceiling. Can you see those shells and sea life remains in this limestone? *(Shutterstock)*

Lessons from the Monacans

Teepees are not found at the Monacan village. *(Shutterstock)*

Monacans lived in wigwams. *(Jennifer Shanks)*

A work shed, constructed of cattails. *(Roanoke Times)*

The Natural Bridge is so important to the Monacan people that they have a visitor's area on the property. The most frequently asked question from visitors is, "Where are the teepees?" There are no teepees. Teepees are common to tribes which are frequently on the move. The Monacans lived

in wigwams constructed of dried and bent wood. Relying more on farming, the Monacans did not follow deer or bison like other tribes farther west. Instead, they remained in Southwestern Virginia.

They value everything in nature and try to avoid any waste. Even the flutes used in their celebrations are made from turkey bones!

The chief's headdress is displayed at the Monacan Indian Nation Museum.

This flute was made from a turkey bone. *(Shutterstock photo illustration)*

Powwows are a way Native Americans pass on their culture. *(Shutterstock)*

Legends and History

The story of the Monacans seeing the bridge materialize at just the right moment is only one of many stories and legends

Believe it or not, a highway runs over the top of the Natural Bridge.

and legends that surround the Natural Bridge. It has long been said

that our first president, George Washington, surveyed the area early in his career. Visitors can walk under the bridge today and see the letters "GW" carved into an inside wall. There, he used a rope to make his way down the wall where he left his initials for future visitors to see. Today, park rangers and others note that the

The initials of GW are carved inside the painted box. Can you see it?

carvings were not discovered until the 1920s.

What is known for certain is that our third president, Thomas Jefferson, saw the site. He was so impressed that in 1774 he reached out to King George III of England and was given permission to purchase the bridge for 20 shillings. That's about $225 in today's money value. What a bargain!

Thomas Jefferson designed his home, Monticello. *(Pixabay)*

Always Learning

It's not surprising that Thomas Jefferson would be so interested in the Natural Bridge. Jefferson spent his life studying and learning as much as he could about the world around him.

He designed and helped create the University of Virginia. He also designed Monticello, his impressive home near Charlottesville. A visit to just the back room of his home tells us much about the man. It is filled with books. It's been said that when he was a student at the College of William and Mary, he would read and study for 15 hours a day. He owned over 6,000 books at a time when a book cost as much as most people would earn working for three full days! Also in this room, you can see his telescope he used to view the world outside. In the center of the room,

Thomas Jefferson designed his study and bedroom for comfort and convenience. *(Carol M. Highsmith, Library of Congress)*

there is an amazing copy machine which allowed him to make a duplicate of anything he wrote.

Jefferson may be best known as a writer, and not just any ordinary writer. He was the man who wrote the Declaration of Independence in 1776. This document declared to the King of England that the American Colonists would no longer live as second-class citizens with no voice in their government.

A gifted and remarkable man, he was like all of us, less than perfect. Modern critics believe that the man who wrote that "all men are created equal" should have done more to eliminate slavery during his Presidency.

Natural Bridge in Art

The Natural Bridge has been painted by many artists from around the world. One in particular was Edward Hicks. Born in Pennsylvania in 1780, Hicks was a Quaker minister and folk artist.

This portrait of Edward Hicks was painted by his cousin Thomas.

Quakers are interested in finding peace with all people and all creatures. Hicks was inspired by the Bible verse found in the 11th chapter of Isaiah that tells of a day when "... wolves will live in peace with lambs, and leopards will lie down to rest with goats. Calves, lions, and young bulls will eat together, and a little child will lead them." From this verse, Hicks painted several pieces that are called the "Peaceable Kingdom."

In one of his most impressive pieces, Hicks combined his vision of peace among animals and

THE PEACEABLE KINGDOM OF THE BRANCH.

The wolf also shall dwell with the lamb & leopard shall lie down with the kid; & the calf & the young lion & the fatling together; and a little child shall lead them.

peace with Native Americans, all taking place beside the beauty and wonder of the Natural Bridge. How fitting that both the Monacans and later Europeans found the Natural Bridge a place of wonder and hope.

Decorative plates are displayed at the Natural Bridge Historic Hotel and Conference Center.

Natural Tunnel

Natural Bridge is so strong that it supports Virginia Highway 11, which allows trucks and cars to run over

its top every day. Farther west in what is known to many as Virginia Coal Country, there is another natural wonder that supports a different mode of transportation.

The Natural Tunnel is a passageway that was formed through a stone mountain in the western part of the state. It is so long and big that

This train, at Natural Bridge State Park, once operated at a nearby theme park.

From a distance, the size of the mountain is easier to see.

a train could pass through it ... and they frequently do.

In the late 1800s, train companies were looking for ways to transport coal across the country. Traveling over steep mountains is impossible with heavy train loads. Blasting through stone mountains was time consuming and could be dangerous and deadly. Imagine the excitement of finding a passage that was nature-made for train travel. The tunnel is 80 feet high and 850 feet long. That's as long as 24 yellow school buses lined up end-to-end.

So how in the world was this amazing tunnel created? Author Tony Scales provides a detailed explanation in his book "Natural Tunnel, Nature's Marvel in Stone." He offered an easier explanation to a television reporter by saying, "If you give Mother Nature enough time, water can leave a big hole in the ground." And that is how it was done. Ground water working throughout the mountain, combined with the pressure of a small river, worked slowly over time to create the natural marvel.

A sky lift takes visitors down to the base of the mountain in order to see the tunnel.

While passenger trains stopped their service in 1939, the tunnel is still actively used by coal trains today. It is also the centerpiece of Natural Tunnel State Park, where visitors can ride a sky lift down the side of the mountain to experience the tunnel up close.

Power of Coal

Coal has been mined in Virginia since the 1700s. The black rock filled with carbon is found in abundance in the southwestern mountains of the state. Coal is used for heating, to power steam engines, and to produce electricity.

Mining coal requires workers to either remove topsoil

An antique postcard shows a steam engine going through the tunnel. *(public domain)*

755. TRAIN LEAVING NATURAL TUNNEL. SOUTHWEST VIRGINIA.

(Shutterstock)

and rock to find the coal or to tunnel underground to find and bring up the coal. Either way, it is dirty, difficult, and dangerous work. While Santa Claus is known to leave a lump of coal in the stockings of children who haven't been nice, he appreciates the hard work of miners. Since the 1940s, Santa has worked with local business leaders to travel on the Santa Train. He rides through coal mining towns and cities, delivering presents to the children of coal miners. His visits bring joy and great memories to families throughout the region.

Natural Chimneys

It's like a scene out of the legends of King Arthur and the Knights of the Round Table. With the shadow of a giant castle in the background, a knight mounts his horse. He lowers his long, sharp lance. Then, at the signal, he races his horse at break-neck speed. But wait a minute; this isn't ancient times. We're not

From this angle, the chimneys resemble a castle.

Mock sword fights are also part of a jousting tournament. *(Medieval Fantasies Company)*

in England. Merlin the Magician didn't transport us back in time. Those giant towers aren't really part of a castle at all.

   In truth, we are in a remote part of Augusta County, somewhere between Staunton and Harrisonburg. What we are witnessing is the oldest continuously held sporting event held in the United States. Since 1821, people have come to this spot to relive the thrill of the ancient sport of jousting. One Civil War officer was said to have competed on the

From this angle, the chimneys do look like giant smoke stacks.

grounds and became known as the "Knight of the Valley."

What draws them to this spot is an amazing formation that is known as the Natural Chimneys. The stone towers resemble chimneys to some. To others, when the sun is starting to set, it looks like the ruins of a medieval castle. The columns rise from 65 to 120 feet from the ground.

These rock ruins, pocketed with small caves, were created by the effects of a prehistoric ocean which was

There are tunnels and caves in the chimneys.

Someone had a great sense of humor when they created this "unnatural" chimney.

once here. When you consider that the closest ocean is a four-hour drive away, it's clear that Virginia has changed over the years.

Today, in addition to hosting annual jousting tournaments, Natural Chimneys is a beautiful park operated by Augusta County. It features camping, picnicking, a pool, and several nature trails. One trail leads to the very top of the Natural Chimneys.

The knights of the round table are shown around the Holy Grail. *(public domain)*

King Arthur

The tale of King Arthur and his group of knights goes back as far as the fifth century. According to tradition, King Arthur dreamed of a world where everyone lived in peace. This would be accomplished through his band of talented and worthy knights. Instead of sitting at a table with King Arthur at the end giving orders, they sat at a giant round table where each knight was able to speak and offer advice to others.

Knights were to be brave, pure, and skilled. One of the ways they proved their skill was through jousting tournaments. Destroying dragons or rescuing those in need earned a knight bonus points.

Fairy Stone Park

Stuart, Virginia, is like other small towns found in the state. It has an old courthouse, a classic theater, and a train depot. Depending on when you visit, you can enjoy their spring Strawberry Festival or their fall Apple Dumpling Festival. What makes Stuart unusual is the enchanted forest just down the road.

According to the legend, the place now called Fairy Stone State Park is the ancient home to a group of fairies who live in the woods. One day, those fairies heard of the death of Jesus and began to cry. Their tears fell onto the small stones scattered all over the park. It was their

Could this strange opening by the home of one of the park's fairies? People have found crystals all around.

Fairystone Pit Stop is the place to park and search for the stones. It's also a great place to pick up a cold drink on a hot day.

tears that transformed those stones into cross-shaped crystals in honor of Jesus.

You may not believe the story of the fairies and their tears, but the stones are absolutely real. If you visit the park, especially after a rain storm, try searching around the tree roots. If you have enough patience, good eyesight, and a little luck, you'll find a fairy stone of your own.

According to the Virginia Department of Conservation and Recreation, the stones are actually staurolite crystals made of iron, aluminum, and silicate. As the Appalachian Mountains were formed, heat and pressure combined to create the crystals. Since the crystals are harder than the surrounding surface of the mountain, they seem to magically appear as other parts of the mountain wash away.

Find the Fairy Stones

Fairy stones are found in many shapes. Can you find a fairy stone in the rocks above or on this cloth? Here are two examples and a guide from the VA Department of Conservation and Recreation to help.

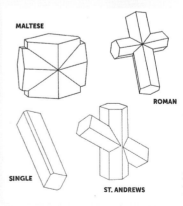

MALTESE

ROMAN

SINGLE

ST. ANDREWS

The Lost City

After searching for fairy stones, be sure to visit the rest of the park. One of the highlights is the beautiful Fairy Stone Lake. As you boat across the lake, it may be hard to believe that you are floating over the top of a lost town.

Fayerdale was a small community founded in 1905 for mining iron and logging in the nearby forests. A train line came directly into town to help transport these products. When selling and manufacturing alcohol became illegal in 1920, the town was also a

The town of Fayerdale rests below this beautiful lake.

The metal used to create the ironclad warship Merrimac came from the area around Fairy Stone Park.

secret location for making "moonshine." The town started to die out with the overlogging of trees and the slowing down of mining operations.

In 1933, it was decided to turn the area into a state park. The remaining residents were moved out and the entire town was flooded to create the lake which is part of the state park.

Imagine a hotel, a blacksmith shop, a train depot, a doctor's office, homes, and even a school all beneath the beautiful Fairy Stone Lake. You'd have to hold your breath pretty well to take lessons at that school!

Fairies and Fairy Tales

Fairy tales and stories of mythical creatures go back to ancient times. Most famously, they have been written about by the Brothers Grimm, the playwright William Shakespeare, and the "Lord of the Rings" author J. R. R. Tolkien.

Some believe that the term fairy only applies to tiny creatures who can fly around with a magic wand and cast spells. "Pinocchio" includes such a fairy that helps the puppet learn the importance of telling the truth and helping others. In the end, he is rewarded by becoming a "real boy."

Many of the stories we now think of as "fairy tales" don't include such magical creatures. Instead, they may have talking

Pinocchio's nose grows every time he tells a lie. He's lucky to have a fairy come to the rescue.

animals like in the story of "Red Riding Hood" or "Goldilocks and the Three Bears."

Some fairy stories are quite scary and violent as in the story of "Sleeping Beauty." An evil fairy promises death to the Princess. Fortunately, she is only placed into a deep sleep from which she is eventually awakened.

And on the subject of waking up, it's certainly nice to wake up and find a gift left by a generous tooth fairy!

Some fairy tales don't feature traditional fairies. Instead they feature fantastic stories with talking animals.

The Dismal Swamp

During the day, Lake Drummond is as peaceful and calm as Fairy Stone Lake. And the surrounding area is full of wildlife. A train of turtles line up on a fallen log. Ducks bob up and down in the water. A beaver lodge can be seen in the distance, and from time to time you can hear a splash from one of the busy creatures.

Calm... peaceful... relaxing... while the sun is out...

But wait. When the sun goes down, this place transforms into something dark, gloomy, and frightening. The vines seem to twist and curl in every direction, a warning that you should have never entered and that you will never escape. The birds have stopped chirping in the distance. Now, every sound seems louder. What is that crackling in the leaves? Perhaps a deer? A bobcat? A black bear?

Now you know why this place is called the Dismal Swamp. It is 113,000 acres of vines and marsh. This wetland system protects one of the largest black bear populations on the east coast.

Swamps or wetlands help absorb rising water during times of heavy rain. The grass rising from the

A black bear mother plays with her cub. Bobcats are sometimes seen in the Dismal Swamp. A group of turtles crowd onto a log. A busy beaver swims. *(all Shutterstock)*

water is very strong and can survive the wind, rain, and changing water levels from the rising and lowering of tides. This grass also filters trash and pollution and keeps it from reaching the lake.

You might notice a rotten smell in the swamp. That smell comes as once living matter, including plants and animal remains, rot and decay. This rotting material becomes detritus (dee-TRITE-us) which provides nutrients for new plant life to grow.

(Author above/Shutterstock below)

Drain the Swamp!

Donald Trump was not the first U.S. president who called on Americans to "Drain the Swamp!" President Trump was talking about an overhaul of Washington, D.C., politics. George Washington, our first president, was hoping to literally drain the entire Dismal Swamp in order to save the land for development. This was at a time when people did not fully appreciate the importance of wetlands. Fortunately, this plan failed. Another plan was more successful. Working with Virginia Governor Patrick Henry, Washington supported a canal system to transport goods and people from Virginia to North Carolina. That canal opened in 1805 and is still in use today.

Maroons

The dangerous work of digging the canal was done by hand by enslaved people in the region. This was not the first time enslaved people made their way to the Dismal Swamp. The U.S. Fish and Wildlife Service shares research that the Great Dismal Swamp became a hideaway for up to 50,000 enslaved people between 1620 and the Civil War.

The people seeking freedom were called "Maroons" which comes from a Spanish word "cimarron" meaning "wild." This referred to their decision to live in this wild, dangerous area, rather than live in the horrible conditions of

A "Maroon" carefully makes his way through the swamp. *(public domain)*

enslavement. The area certainly was wild. The families had to live among the snakes, mosquitoes, and overgrowth. They had to live with the constant fear of discovery by those who would return them to enslavement.

Imagine how creepy this can be as the sun goes down.

Despite all, the Maroons created entire hidden communities deep in the swamp. They found islands where they could build homes. They even learned how to trade with trusted members of the outside world.

The courage and determination of these families and their time in the Great Dismal Swamp is now recognized as part of the National Underground Railroad Network to Freedom.

A Railroad? Underground?

Now, don't go to the Dismal
Swamp hoping to see a train and
underground railroad tracks. The
Underground Railroad was a system
created to help enslaved people escape.

Secrecy was essential to protect the people trying
to run away. The system featured many of the terms
found in the railroad business. "Conductors" would
serve as guides to people hoping to be free. These
people were the "agents." Safe hiding places were
called "stations." While most people dreamed of
making their way to Northern states or Canada, others
found a new life in the depths of the Dismal Swamp.

A name often associated with the Underground
Movement is Harriet Tubman. Enslaved in Maryland,
she escaped and followed the North Star to
Pennsylvania, where she was free. But she was not
happy there. Without her family and friends, she did
not feel totally free. So, she returned to the South
and led at least 13 missions that rescued her family
and friends and helped 70 others make their way to
freedom.

The Great Falls

The Great Dismal Swamp can be a place filled with quiet danger. We now travel north to find a louder kind of danger. In Fairfax County, we hear the Potomac River crashing loudly down rock walls to create the Great Falls that separate Virginia and Maryland.

It's an impressive and easy site to see from three look out points managed by the National Park Service. If you want to get closer, it requires a rather difficult climb over huge boulders and slippery rock walls. It quickly becomes clear that a boat has no chance against the jagged rocks that reach out at the bottom of the falls.

It's also easy to see why George Washington and others determined there must be a safer way to travel the Potomac River. He surveyed the area back in the 1750s and must have already started to think of a solution. After the Revolutionary War, he championed the idea of creating a canal system that would allow smaller craft to avoid the damaging falls.

These were the days before trucks and trains.

(Shutterstock)

Water was the preferred way to move goods from the Ohio River Valley to Virginia. But the plan would require Virginia to work with Maryland. It would be an "interstate" project, the first interstate project created after the founding of our country. George Washington was able to get both states to agree to the project, and a canal company was formed.

Unlike the canal in the Dismal Swamp, this canal worked by means of a series of chambers, called locks, that were built beside the falls and dangerous parts of the river. Water could be forced to flow into and then

Here are the remains of the locks. These channels by-passed the falls.
The locks were filled with water to move boats around the dangerous rocks.

out of each lock,
raising and lowering
a boat and its cargo
along the way. This
movement slowly
happened one lock
or chamber at a
time.

While Washington did not live to see the opening
of the canal, it did become the success he dreamed

it would be. Thousands of boats would bypass the dangerous falls every year, safely transporting sugar, flour, corn, wheat, and many other products. Eventually other waterways and then other forms of transportation took over, but you can still see the remains of the locks today.

While the canal started as a vision from George Washington and others, its construction was the work of others, including enslaved people from the area who were forced to do the dangerous and difficult work. One such enslaved man used his resourcefulness to move from enslaved worker to freed superintendent and engineer of the project.

George Pointer was born in 1773. At the age of 13 he was "rented" to the canal company to help build the canals. He was present as the land was surveyed for the project and quickly learned what was necessary to build and maintain a working canal. Along the way, he was able to earn enough money to secure his own freedom.

When the supervising engineer for the canal project retired, it was Pointer's ability to observe and learn new skills that earned him that position. Perhaps

his proudest moment came when he and his granddaughter Mary Ann ferried President John Quincy Adams safely across the Potomac River.

As huge as the Great Falls are, perhaps more amazing is the number of times the falls have "disappeared." This marker shows the height of water far above the top of the falls. The highest flood recorded was in 1936.

This post shows the dates and height of floods in the Great Falls area.

The Chesapeake Bay

Once we get past the Great Falls and continue down the Potomac River, we can make our way to the biggest natural treasure in this book. It is a treasure we share with the state of Maryland. It is the Chesapeake Bay, the largest estuary in the United States. An estuary is a place where fresh water from rivers and streams combines with the salt water of the nearby ocean. Over 150 rivers and streams flowing from six states make their way into the bay.

It is a huge water basin over 200 miles long and up to 30 miles wide, covering over 4,000 square miles.

Before its "discovery" by European settlers, it was the home to Native American tribes who settled near its shores. Perhaps the most famous of these people was led by Chief Powhatan, the father of Pocahontas. They called the place the "Chesepiooc" which translated to "Great Shellfish Bay." The bay is certainly known world-wide for its crabs, clams, and oysters.

While he was not the first European to see the Chesapeake Bay, Captain John Smith spent two years traveling and mapping the land and waters surrounding the bay. He said, "Heaven and earth never agreed better to frame a place for man's habitation... Here are mountains, hills, plains, valleys, rivers, and brooks, all running into a fair bay."

Captain John Smith was one of the original English explorers who settled in Jamestown, Virginia. The colonists lived in a wooden fort built in wetlands near the James River.

It is amazing how Captain John Smith could create detailed maps without a drone or some other way to see from high above.

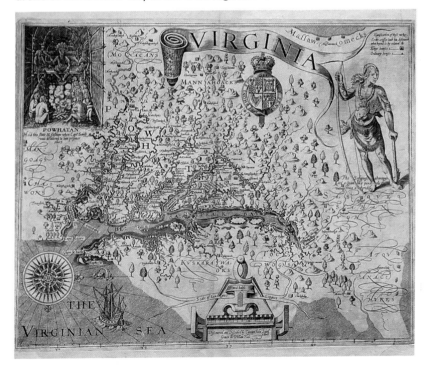

Alyssa Jones holds this puppet version of Pocahontas, all dressed up to see the King of England. All of this is based on the classic image shown on the right, similar to the classic image of John Smith shown on the left.

Captain John Smith

Captain John Smith's relationship with Pocahontas is legendary. While they never married one another, their lives are forever linked. Their most famous story tells how Pocahontas saved John Smith from Powhatan, her father. She offered her life in place of his. Some historians believe the story may be a myth created by John Smith for his later writings. Either way, Pocahontas remains a beloved woman who sought peace between her people and those from England. It is certainly true that John Smith's writings and maps did much to gain support and interest in Virginia and the Chesapeake Bay.

Pirates of the Bay

With over 1,800 shipwrecks in the Chesapeake Bay, you might expect a fair share of pirates hunting for sunken treasure. It's true that many a pirate came into the bay ... but you might be surprised at what many of those pirates were looking for. It wasn't gold. It was oysters! And they weren't hunting those oysters for their pearls. The oysters of the Chesapeake Bay aren't known for producing beautiful pearls. They are known by many to be really delicious.

Harper's Magazine showed the Oyster Pirates at night.

The Rainbow Puppet Pirates are searching for pearls. Most pearls found in Chesapeake Bay oysters are small and have uneven color.

After the Civil War, the oysters of the Chesapeake Bay became desired by folks all up and down the East Coast. Soon, fisherman from New England came with big boats and dredged or scooped huge amounts of oysters out of the bay. This harmed the small local businesses and families that made their living using long tongs to bring up oysters. Maryland and Virginia outlawed these "Oyster Pirates." Virginia Governor William Cameron himself joined in the fight to keep illegal fishermen from the bay. These "Oyster Wars" could become dangerous at times as local fishermen worked to protect their way of life.

The bay is more than just oysters. It serves as a nursery for many other amazing creatures. You might find sea turtles, dolphins, sharks, and fish in the

A bald eagle stands guard over the bay. Blue crabs are found in the bay. A red fox hides in the underbrush. A deer family hides among the nearby trees. *(all Shutterstock)*

waters. In the air you might see bald eagles, owls, vultures, and ducks. In the surrounding wetlands you might spot deer, coyote, fox, and maybe a black bear.

The bay is so inviting, it occasionally gets a visit from a curious Florida manatee. When you consider that manatees typically swim only three to five miles an hour, the 900-mile trip is quite a feat.

The most famous manatee visitor was named Chessie, in tribute to the bay. Since his first visit in

the 1990s, he has been the subject of books, a musical, and news coverage. And who can blame him for visiting again and again? When you consider its size, the Chesapeake Bay is Virginia's biggest treasure!

By the way, the reach of the bay is much farther than you might imagine. The Chesapeake Bay Watershed, which includes any waterway that makes its way into the bay, covers 64,000 square miles. It includes six states as far away as New York, and it includes 60% of Virginia. That means that water from way past Charlottesville, Lynchburg, or Winchester can make its way to the bay. That also means that pollution and trash that gets in our water from those remote locations can have an

Chessie the Manatee is depicted in print, onstage, and in the news.

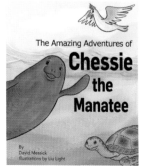

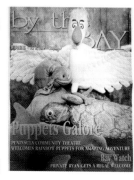

impact on the safety of every creature in the bay. It's up to many communities and many people to protect this enormous treasure.

From the air, you can better see how huge the Chesapeake Bay is. *(NASA)*

(Shutterstock)

How did the Bay Form?

In 1983, scientists found evidence that a giant meteor crashed into a spot that is now the "mouth" or opening of the Chesapeake Bay. The very bright meteor is called a bolide.

The meteor did not actually scoop out or form the bay immediately. Instead, by crashing into the earth, the meteor began the process of forming the bay. According to David Powars, one of the scientists who discovered the crater, "Within minutes, millions of tons of water, sediment, and shattered rock were cast high into the atmosphere for hundreds of miles along the East Coast."

As we discovered with the creation of the Natural Chimneys and the Natural Bridge, Virginia has changed over the years. Where seas once existed, now we have stone towers and a mighty bridge. Where the meteor hit, we now have the giant Chesapeake Bay.

A Final Word...

Well, we've reached the end of another adventure. Perhaps the most amazing thing about these treasures is that every one of them was created, at least in part, by little drops of water.

Rain drops accumulated and filled the waterways that created the Natural Tunnel, Natural Chimneys, Natural Bridge, and the lake and waterways of the Dismal Swamp. Rain helps create the Potomac River that becomes part of the Great Falls and later fills the Chesapeake Bay. Rain water washes away rocks to reveal Fairy Stones. Rain drops find their way underground, bringing minerals that create the impressive columns and formations in the Virginia caverns.

One little drop of water may not seem like much. You might barely notice it when a rain shower is starting to fall. But one little raindrop combined with another, and then another, can accomplish great things.

That makes me think of you and me. When we work together with our friends and neighbors, we can accomplish amazing things, too. We can accomplish things we might not be able to do on our own. We can bring happiness to those who are sad. We can feed folks who are hungry. We can work on projects that make the places where we live even better. I can't wait to see the amazing things you and your friends do.

(Shutterstock)

Partial Bibliography

Edwards, Roberta. (2009) Who Was George Washington? New York: Penguin Workshop.

Fradin, Dennis (2003) Who Was Thomas Jefferson? New York: Penguin Workshop.

Gerth, Joseph. "For 76 Years, the Santa Train has delivered Christmas to Appalachia." Courier-Journal.com, November 29, 2018, Accessed October 22, 2023.

Scales, Tony. (2004) Natural Tunnel, Nature's Marvel in Stone. Johnson City: The Overmountain Press.

Spencer, Edgar W. et al. (2019) Guide to Natural Bridge State Park and The Caverns at Natural Bridge (Fourth Edition). Lowell: Poorhouse Mountain Press.

Thanks

Sue Elliott, Monacan Indian Nation Cultural Foundation.

Susan Finta, National Parks Service Ranger, Great Falls Park.

Jan Gilliam, Assistant Curator of Exhibits, Colonial Williamsburg Foundation.

Kenneth Horowitz, Chief Ranger Visitor Experience, Natural Bridge State Park.

Danny Martin, Park Ranger – Interpreter, Fairy Stone State Park.

Joe Proctor, Vice President and General Manager, Shenandoah Caverns.

Diana Slagell and Lily Whitman, Town of Grottoes, Grand Caverns.

Lya Walker, General Manager, Natural Bridge Historic Hotel and Conference Center.

Jennifer Shanks, Caverns Supervisor and Larry Wheeler, Caverns Manager, The Caverns at Natural Bridge.

And the staff at Natural Chimneys Regional Park and Natural Tunnel State Park.

Glossary

accumulate - To gather or collect.

Algonquins - One of the largest groups of Native Americans in North America.

anthodite - Needle-like crystals that point out from one spot.

carbon - A natural element that forms coal, gas, and diamonds.

cavern - A large cave.

excavate/excavating - To find or remove things by digging.

formations - A development, sometimes of rocks or cave shapes.

fossil - Evidence of ancient plants or animals, like teeth or bones.

geologist - A scientist who studies the Earth's surface, especially the rocks.

Great Depression - 1929 to 1939 when many US people had little work, food, or money.

impressive - Something that excites or draws attention.

joust/jousting - A battle between two knights on horseback.

knight - Skilled soldiers from long ago in Europe.

limestone - A rock that is made from pieces of animal shells.

Monacans - A Native American tribe, recognized and found in Virginia.

Quakers - A religious group that works to create peace with others.

stalactites - A cave formation hanging from the ceiling.

stalagmites - A cave formation that rises from the floor.

staurolite - A mineral that may form into the shape of a cross.

survey/surveyed - To gather information, like the height, length, and shape of land areas.

urchin - An underwater creature with spines that stick out.

Books from Rainbow Puppets

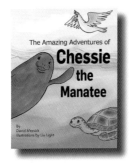

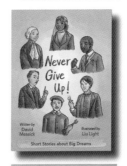

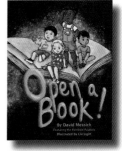

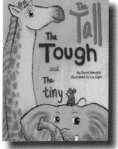